AF504086

MICHAEL SCHMIDT

BEDLAM & THE OAKWOOD

essays on various *fictions*

"I want awfully . . . to see if there is anything to be got out of a gondola."

Henry James

This book is dedicated to Sir Maurice Bowra

Previous collections by Michael Schmidt include:
Black Buildings (Carcanet Press)
It was my Tree (Anvil Press)

Acknowledgement is due to the editors of *Stand, Outposts, Workshop, Isis, Carcanet,* and *Slant*. Three poems from this collection have appeared in a broadsheet, *Bedlam and the Oak-Wood*, in the Sycamore Press.

Printed at Compton Press, Compton Chamberlayne, Salisbury, Wilts.

SBN 902145 13 4

Copyright: © Carcanet Press
      Pin Farm
      South Hinksey
      Oxford.
      1970

CONTENTS

PART I

BIOGRAPHIES

"My heart, imprisoned in a hopeless isle..."
Drayton

Dreams
for Alan Ward

Some poets dream better than others.
A few court the sea-lark, fire
the ideal sail, and come back free,
landward on a wave, to inspire
dark colleges in marble. That's Shelley.
Those provoked by landscape usually tire
of ecstasy, shrivel into platitudes of duty.

Romantics, you know, wear out
with dreaming — die young, or join
the old to lie slumberless, probing
hexametrically the lack of pain
where the old hurt was burning,
their heart's eye melted to a mere
chest. But those appalling

tinkers who never close their eyes
but scrutinize each rhyme and grind
each syllable, once at least are burst on
by a true dream. Chaucer, you find,
one time only asleep in his green-
house dreamed an eagle: the clawed hand
of a violet snatched him up
and blinded him with stars.

Jonathan Swift's Body

Poor Swift — to have had flesh. Nothing
stung him worse than that. Caped in black
he floated over Dublin cobbles, playing
at form. But body was there. To be oak
in the woods — or on a Winter meadow feeling
as the Winter horses free, long mane
and flight through pale sun —

no. He might keep a stable for his mind
to choose its palfrey, gallop in a wood
that catches Irish wind
as wings do. But night would
whip his candle in a closed room, find
in bursts of flame where hair and white
flesh were: gooseflesh at the sight.

Snufting — then dark brought
ugly naked things that burst and ran,
to suppurate in dreams bright
as the candle made him. Then

the unexpected calm of forests came;
in sleep he grew rigid. Now! but the body
won't die. It lasts. Servants maim
and prod the vision in a clouding eye.

Let the lumberjack whom Milton would not name
bring his two-edged axe,
chop the dean now! The body
won't die though. It lasts.

Samuel Johnson's Marriage

The clumsy schoolmaster married
a widow twice his age; is now awake
to the wry dog-star.

At the keyhole night-shirted scholars
take turns. The mind without equal
is discovering its grotesque body
by candlelight. Not iambic
rhythm. Those little boys giggle
next day behind Herodotus.

Turn more to words. You are no bee,
Sam Johnson, to stray among flowers.

There is time to unlearn
and learn the graceless get beauty
out of words or fantasy. Give
the dusty urchin as he sleeps a copper,
and at midnight howl out with Lear
how one with many kingdoms

gave them to thankless daughters:
mind and body.
How no Cordelia brings a healing hand.

Hatching

for Jon Stallworthy

If Rimbaud had not died of amputation,
he would have died of cancer of the lip
because he smoked clay pipes. Nothing finally
held him down — certainly not song. Verlaine
kept on deathless, a soul in bandages,
sang or cried out still occasionally
under his breath.

But the man excommunicant from dreams
(this we must believe) goes somehow up
to heaven as he dries. Opium, arak, or drab
sodomy in London breaks the dark-shell world
for the incubant to rise, brace its silence
on clean air. Rimbaud had long purgatory

before hatching. Deserts undertook him in the shell.
Inch-deep he carved his name in Luxor granite
where desert-swallows nest. And he sold
exquisite slaves. Walking the Egyptian fire
he kept his mouth shut — or in prose. Some say
Ethiopian angels paced the furnace with him: love
was then shell-dry, the heaven gate wide open.

Mr. James

Shutters against Summer,
chairs under sheets, and an all-
yellow garden. I have touched only
the writing desk and stool.
Outside, the gold rose, its teeth
hung on a stem. The sea.

Dim must: gasp
and the bamboo fans
have not air enough
to give you breath. Tonight
stars pump an atmosphere of sea-rose.

Here as blue oysters we characters
are open to an irritant that fails us.
Occasionally we achieve a petulant sublime.

Below, the old sea-keeper
sleeps beside his sea, his hull
carrying coral troves deeper.
As we sat talking
our spirits went to bed.

Voices all night cherish
one another side by side
and never touching. Don't,
for you cannot, follow the spirits
to sleep, or touch them.
Beauty and they are the sea-bed.

Nailed like Stoats

You chose the Ouse, with pebbles
in your pockets and your hat well
knotted on with scarves. It was
Ophelia for an ugly woman,
ending in the sea.

Up high in silent curtains
constrained whimpering of birds
and two low voices calling at each other.
One: revile the ocean.
One: live unaware you live.

Around you the suppliant
generosity to gifted invalids —
a lifetime of it. Critics were kept at bay.
Your correspondence was meticulously edited.
Hostility came from the Spring

in gnarled roses, aphids swarmed your
children and the noon, devouring light.
Rainclouds sucked dry all stems and blew
elsewhere, until the garden was sand, and
you were free to choose the ocean way.

Tagore

for Alexandra, Nicholas, and Harold Seddon

At ten he first journeyed from Calcutta
towards the mountains. Before, the only trees
were hacked with love-notes, slogans, a few
blue leaves. Men resembled them. On the road,
as houses disappeared, space, and everywhere,
he saw, was not a den of bodies.

Long grass, uncropped woods, the sun-fields;
waterfalls became more than the stonefalls
of the great hotels, and glass. A growth —
mountains yawned at his approach, took
him up, new hands. He forgot
whole hours the black hole, complicated alleys,

in a road where water-oxen drew gold loads.
Great peaks raised his eye beyond the most
aspiring bird's flight, until the sky
seemed possible and blue,
then let down the child in waterfalls,
through willows to a new kind of sleep.

He came back to Calcutta. Enough
he learned of colour and the sun
to recognize the earth his city stood on.
Human forms became like mountain forms:
one could conceive how possible a sky
would be above them, given breathing space.

That Man Lowell

Notes on the Notebook

The plot gulped
every human chance.
First it followed seasons, then
took charge, took snow and made it burn.
No room now but energy, too many
faces to pick one out for lover.

That's the way with fictions:
where settlers return, having scalped
the last recalcitrant redskin. The land
goes upside-down, and Winter slides a knife
through the new cottages.
Then vague impish noises in the grass,
the slow, hallucinatory Summer —

when the accountant comes, sweating
in verse, tallying, making heroes
of the most accurate tinkers.
Or else he sees the plot within himself,
throws rhyme away and turns upon the land
with fire and sonnets which
are not Petrarchan.

He gives: a garden where
each flower is caused to ramble,
every face is shaded by a parasol.
"Almost all this life has been
good to me. I see my face refracted
through the symmetry of fountains."

The task done, he believes no more
in pain, the red scarred trees,
or territory where armies passed
and monuments were set up
and pulled down.

PART II

SETTINGS

"a hopeless isle,
Peopled with armies of pale jealous eyes..."
Drayton

B

Letter

to Robert Burns Shaw

I was considering your ploughman cousin,
that well of unconscious celebration, harrowing
in ballads behind an addled drey. If I could imitate
his brogue I would send you an account. But where
lies kinship between you? What mouse or hay-seed
runs your common blood — a cousin, for
all that, is a cousin.

Maybe you're geminian cousins, polarized by time.
Maybe you're having us on. But speculation is never
so charming as your parallel biographies.

He learned rhythm from the horse-hoof fumbling
stone, crack of rook wings on a crisp sky,
the gypsy balladeer. You, two centuries later, know
neither horse nor bird, only dry syllables, a dusty
window and a firescape suggesting unlikely adventure;
images of human pain or passion —

anything that would improve on that
not-life among cobwebs, that hissing kettle,
and never rain to wet you to the skin.

Luncheon

Over green rice, let us think of Japan. Today
so many British poets go — after real mountains,
cedars like pagodas, or palaces of Kyoto
resembling pines. The people: pacific, hospitable.

At home in our green rice, contemplate
emigrating to so sensible and prosperous a nation,
as it builds, rebuilds — situated like a most diligent
coral polyp in the gentle map-blue of the China Sea.
The diet we share today with every Japanese
is what the earliest emperor
tasted in his jasmine lodge, sipping haiku.

But one cannot help hearing Takahashi,
in his toy atomic nautilus, open old scars
in the ocean floor, cry out to small beasts of the Orient:
a voice like sculpted fire, but too isolated
in his history to accuse. Someone
had to hold the camera up
to Nagasaki. Now sediment and animals seem true.

Japan has been accurately rebuilt so that
to an outsider the new is the old — down to the diet.
But the rebuilders know what an eye is made of
under tears, and running shadows charred to a wall.

Venice: a letter to Robert Browning
for Elizabeth Jennings

About Venice I shall tell you only what
impressed me. What can you do today
in a gondola? Now the water-rats are fat
as Doge's profiles, scampering and businesslike
on horizontal boathouse doors, rippling
thick water with dragged tails.

Romance is out of wet alleys. The sea
has made a sloppy wedding with a gabled land.
Worst, the inhabitants succumbed long ago,
in particular their ancient poet who, still
inexorable, forgets his language and in lunacy
wades knee-deep beneath the Jew's black bridge.

In sleep I saw a place as you said it was,
as it might have been, but cannot be.
The gondolier's tune is not Galuppi, spat
from the depth of his throat in the salt below
San Rocco. What would Canaletto do
with the charred sky-line? This is Venice,

yonder is her sea, Tyrian blue, the shade
Astarte's eyes —. But when I spoke
to that old poet in his wading by the bridge
he replied so calmly in silence,
I understood, and tell you
your city is already less than dead.

At Padua

The other day in Padau I encountered the gardener
who tends trees in Europe's oldest botanical park.
Formed like Giotto's Joseph, drab and large, he was
a living sympathy in space, bent towards a tree.
He could not afford entry to the Scrovegni chapel,
and had not appreciated himself aesthetically.

Since my Italian is not, and he spoke Latin tags
and little English, we only looked at one another.
Fingering his spade, he fed parings from his thumbnail
to a robin. In a ginko tree a blackbird sang

and this man was a temple. As if
to stand were not enough, he picked a spray
of blue plumbago and handed it — I received,
and left, one of his birds, perched
on that fine flower, which I keep, and shall,
pressed in my guidebook to Padua.

The Wisdom of the Sleeper at the Opera

If you're afraid of falling
asleep at the opera, think of this:
music makes astounding dreams of sleep —
how the Commendatore's statue moves
through violins, draws on your inside eye
the image of all Erinny's, that bear your
lecherous soul below deep Hell;

or Brünhilde brings
Belsen in a cry.

And you start awake to the lighted scene
in a dark House — looking on,
abruptly innocent of plot, except the plot
you dreamed. No audience witnessed what you
have seen, the audience's soul in sleeping,
and your own. For fear of breaking out of fictions
any more, you prop your eyelid open till the interval.

Inside the Mapmaker's Mind

Shallows. Deep, the deep-sea tugging seaweed,
seaweed curling currents on her fingers. How
should I reveal? Between latitude slats the world
looks up, stalks her names and mountains behind bars.

Icebergs, one again last night, burst the diagrammatic
ocean, catch a river mouth and choke the water back on
the blue land: then shifting, melt to green.

This is too cold, too pastel. The world would contour,
my pencil smooths it down. It would make peninsulas
be faces, toes, or fists — some evidence that men
inhabit there, that in its pacing behind bars it is not
amorphous. I keep to the rules, manipulating

my latitudes to cut long names, eye-spots of large
cities into halves. The smoke I breathe out circumscribes
my patch of globe, which struggles as I trace.

No men are visible, and what they did
or do is letters only, salted on the land. My smoke
irritates Cuba, Mexico, the Caribbean. But my pencil pays
no toll, wanders each road unafraid of bandits, prisoners.

Cyclone Garden

Purple cyclones on dull storm-cloud,
three at once, come leap-frog
over Arkansas. Here it is incredibly
still, like a place near angry flowers.

Watch them: they won't move this way.
They go for towns, not cottages, follow
the telephone wires from gulch to gulch, on
to Little Rock where windows stand
open to receive them.

Trees are the petals, bursting upward
in the flower, or tumble-weed from Mexico
rolls in them like seed:

so the wind takes on a body as it can,
and like all bodies becomes violent,
lurches north eager to give distant gifts,
but always clumsy as it comes, breaking.

Castle

I am most curious about Duncan's rumoured
ghost. Tense for sleep, servants tell,
he paces his sky battlement till dawn
in fleur-de-lys pyjamas. The Great Bear
tells no tale against a soul. This
is the place Macbeth made black,
crenelated replica of hell. All sound
is landscape sound, crickets gagged
by drizzle, woods marching on the sea.

Among treacherous mail-shirts (each scale
with a sting) I've spent twenty years —
half of them an infant. I never
came on the ghost or king:
it's suddenly time to ask
the raw fortress man-to-man,
how far are you going to let
the fiction take you?

A tudor made a feudal intrigue,
poured each stone full of rumours
not to be purged, that run
like the liquid tick of a clock.
Fiction has set voices in metal helmet jaws.
Ivy, crawling rook-wings, and the rainfall:
a long time I took this for horizon.
Now I think I'll meet the lady walker
in her sleep who tells illuminating tales.

PART III

SOME FICTIONS

"... The shores beset with thousand secret spies,
(My Heart) must pass by air, or else die in exile."
Drayton

Bedlam and the Oak-Wood

All day it has been windy. I have stayed
indoors, reading about the lunatics of Bedlam.
They, to undo the tempest that preyed
on their souls practiced acupuncture, some
with mess-knives, others with a toothpick
to the flesh — or to the eye.
When blood ran, the sick
would cry out "blood of charity!"

Some made (I read as the wind
blew) large holes in their wrists, inserting
sprigs of grass or dandelion, rind
of oranges, pretending
they were gardens, that their
bodies could nourish fruit or flower.

Apparently their cold eyes wrung money
out of you. If you gave nothing, you
were splattered with urine, blood; if free
with coppers they kissed your foot, you
could not get away, but gave again.

Wild trees this evening recall them,
entangling your eye, and break —
what oak,
when mountain winds surprise it,
can sustain a simple moonrise?

Mandeville's Book

Surpassing all lands is that most worthy book-
land called Promise, afloat in Jesu's blood.
Holy Mary, bread and wine. He took flesh,
encumbered him and lived there —

Mandeville. Better pierce his dream
of history than burst his anonimity.
Unknown liars cease to lie, become
poetical — our sort of men: not men.

You want knowledge from his territory.
I am after marvels — griffons, hippo-
centaurs true as tapestry. Together we
will beget a wisdom here.

To begin, god's plenty
is our great mother, Mary Earth.
We deface her body
with our feet and habergeons.

For a purifying instant put faith
in unarmed fancy, rebuild her youth
with dreams. After all, the world is round
for some. Columbus took Mandeville to bed

those last days before landfall, whispered
with him stories of an east unknown.
We shall find out the dog-head man,
the dame with breasts like basilisks

and prove our mother fecund beyond
mere fact. Written word turns always
banana tree and found a symbol of the Cross.
towards a truth. His probed the dim

No thing is impossible. Those men
whose heads grow in their armpits he
brought above ground, while Dante cowered
with them under mountains. All

is light: this richest territory
afloat in Jesu's blood, called Promise,
gives us more than simple dreams. We
will clean our Maria of facts.

Appendix

I am reading the appendix to Arthur's
Book of Hours, pressing my hand to a list
of sacred taboos, benign stars, effective curses.
Here the rollick, the nightmare, of ancestors.

Concealed in parchment, sly areas of
old monastic grins and fingerprints,
footprints of the devil masked as goat.
Envy jockeys a green hound, and Avarice,
mole-blind, fixes her claws
on the gold genitals of youth.

Worst is Hell:
an unspeakably beautiful lady orders roses
in the anus of her knightly lover. Flame.
This reading leaves me seated
in the gateway to some unlosable wisdom,
and here at least I am no cynic. Descent
of angels through the roof like dancing marionettes,
through the floorboards ugly spearheads glower,
and old familiars slap their sides that times
are not much altered: the hand
of flesh still traces immortal ugliness.

Dog

for Barry Morse

At Paestum recently, Praxiteles' memorial dog
was unearthed — all bone, breathless. Though
not yet authenticated, it is, archaeologists agree,
that artist's final work, stunned by new light,
not yet admired enough to bark.

Pedestalled among olives in an imagined colonnade,
it curls for cameramen. At night it's closely guarded,
no longer watch-dog but dog watched.
Wind can make up burglars in the grove, stars do
their clockwork, but it sleeps even to full moons.

On its flank, marble cracked at moisture and the slug.
No wonder the sculptor was frightened at the mere
stone of his monument. In old age he lost all passion
for fleshy Grecian forms, exchanged them
for a hollow-ribbed dog in regardless sleep.

Its lying expressed the old man's studio, smell
of straw, inertia of the moths — silence excavation
cannot plumb. All that heard its barking, even willows
of the sea, sleep in its bones. That Paestum bought
and buried it substantiates the irony.

Archaeologists

at Tell-el-Amarna, for the Hoppes

We dug a year to find the mummy in her
pyramid, mummy-cloth intact, the sepulchre
offerings untampered. In her chamber we reach
conclusions about funerals, preservation, each
mortuary habit in Amenophus IV's brief dynasty.

In his time, Egyptians carved iconography
like life. Ugly and gentle found place in art,
even a split nose, or a real death-mask; inert
early gods and Pharaohs were dead as their stone.
Amenophus' sculptors made granite flesh and bone.

That's why the new tomb raised the hair,
even on scientists' heads, to bristle. There
was a maiden in scintilla drapes, and breathing
virginal, madonnal; we came whispering
as if to church, our awe

like Thoth's anchorites', who at a distance saw
her, their sibyl. Somewhere as lions go,
magnificent to weariness, she had come
here, and still no place to rest away from
eyes. After closer inspection, however, we know

nothing was special about her. In method
her buriers preserved tradition, a silver
plug to stop her mouth, gold amulets on each finger.
Worst, they actually beautified the dead,
rearranged her face, even plastered

over a cicatrice along her forehead,
where in the dog-trance, harrowing her soul
she fell into the pit and screamed of future war.
(That is what the walls tell.)
Analyzed, we found the brain, to keep the skull
from rot, was dissolved with acid,
and sucked out at the nostril by a straw.

Watchers

All night I have sat up, keeping
madness from your door — difficult,
especially in Mexico, where demons use
catholic techniques, walk through walls
familiarly: pale Andromache with child
last night bathed you in tears: they were salt.
Rats sound in the thatch like nails.

I use broomstick, a ceramic Virgin Mary,
a squat candle and a ram's horn — the local custom —
say charms, nod off sleep so you can sleep.
The devil plagues selectively — never touches me.
Subtle he is too, plays pagan to my pagan, snufts
my candle, and all remedy is vain:

in your window palms bleed the moon, wind-swayed.
The day you spent with ruins brings at night the god
of ruin, broken bones; perhaps the god whose tongue
is made of feathers, too, who grinds us with his blood,
reshapes us, gives cold fire to all our eyes.
Your never-sleeping guardian is as good as dead:
one night you called me ruin out of dream.

Lazarus at the Seaside

Wet newspapers revolve in gull wings,
set to sea. One roar in the castle's ear —
calm, long. His body: polka-dot bandages
and beach-towels, half-asleep, learning
how worlds slow, lose moons, fall
gently free to stars Sea-sound
is like star-sound. Motion
ends in that perpetual
tide-like exhalation.
All pain goes out.

And the demented beach-ballers come;
their team leader, crass against the sand,
hitches up his towel. Lesser creatures throng
in mute obeissance. Only one voice.
Lazarus perceives its whistle glowing
in his ear, fierce, unrelenting. To come
so close to sleep, then wake,
hot sand in your eye:
the eternal sea crawls down.

A Word about my Friend Herrera

This time last year Herrera took
cyanide in Delhi. His letters as he sailed east
the long way from Southampton now look
like folded sails. "Each ocean requires a feast
of its own for calm," he wrote — the Atlantic drank
cool north lights; the evening Pacific tasted
plankton, brightened as the whale sank
its candle wings. In Fiji brown women wasted
the whole day for the ocean, naked, warm —
a two-month calm.

But when the China Sea sipped down
junks of tea and yellow men
his mind turned. The letters frown
as the boat harbours in Ceylon:
the Indian Ocean. He had seen
enough death and storm when
that omnivore joined lips with filthy
Ganges, and a body

bumped his hull like a dud mine.
At midnight in Delhi he saw the sign
of the goat's hoof, heard the gull-man call,
folded the last sail. This sail.
Death was a cadence fall
to almond, sandalwood.

Credo

for the Great Fictions

These dark scenarios, I will remind you,
are Elsinore, and there are ghosts about.
You sleep here with Gertrude
and footlights. For several months, four hours,
a purple river overruns your bland day.

Architectured light draws out
mass executions by sword, and chalice
always lipped with poison. See where mist
crawls from the ocean, moon flowers
open their pale mouths. Above this mild

articulation of the night, ugly men
take the ugly on. How is it done?
Efficiently. Ophelia drowns on air
and with the talking flowers — almost
imperceptible the crawling mist.

And if the ugly dampens us as well, dark scenes
creep out of the theatre, follow us home
in a separate cab, and crawl in at the window
as we sleep, think how we are made the stage
and, critical, the atmosphere reviews us.

PART IV

SOME MORE FICTIONS

"He framed him wings with feathers of his thought,
Which by their nature learned to climb the sky;
And with the same he practicèd to fly,
Till he himself this eagle art had taught . . ."
Drayton

Airborne

for Elizabeth Thomas

Cruising above the Gulf of Mexico, if you looked
carefully, you could see the caravelles
a first time touching land. Despite
the drone of engines, a seaman's voice
sights Hispaniola: spears shake at the sea-edge,
guns are trained towards shore, until the red-faced
gods pitch flag and tent, "for Isabel and Christ!"

Each time I travel home they are there
on the fringe of America, followed by ranks
of buccaneers. Airborne is to be bird
off land, off time, in the sunset's eye.
Beneath you what is lives its full life for you.

Popocatépetl, the broken giant's throat,
heaves tails of cloud, and his sleeping
Iztaccihuatl wears white evening stars
upon her breasts. Raw glare from Lake Tezcoco
slices the mountain legend

with history. In the spiked island city
the Aztec danced — airborne, you hear Cuauhtemoc
tortured in his feet cry louder in silence
than vanquished Montezuma. Before touchdown,
reckon how a place can hand its future to you also,
like a gift, if you are looking; how the conquered will
turn, knives in their fists, white-faced and weeping.

The New Volcano

Yesterday a village near Puebla registered
earthquakes, fissured earth, stink of sulphur
in hot spigots from the ground; how ash and smoke
deepened like black snow. There is a history:

Paricutín burst this way — a farmer ploughed,
sowed corn, and reaped a red volcano, lava rock,
a buried township and two cremated oxen.
Indians are much preoccupied with death now,

with the way Popocatépetl shadows and conspires
above them in his low wavering smoke-line —
once a mere plateau of cactuses. Why should
the old myth from before baptism and the potsherd

of a church (whose bells the shaking earth can ring
or silence) not be true: that earth is a seed sprouting
abrupt flowers, turning over fruit of stone?
According to the village priest, prospects of desolation

bend the Indian mind back on old ritual.
Hares, excessive cactus-wine, are sacrificed;
an infant's blood was sown in two long furrows,
its black hair left to wind, its bones

deposited in flowing water, and its flesh consigned
to fire. When the earth bursts, the flower
will bear the child's name, reverence
due to stone at the birth of stone.

At Nautla

By megaliths of sun, at Nautla — ruins
precariously near the smoking mountain
and the sudden river of Lizard's Eye —
spinners twist cotton on bone needles,
ceramic whorls revolve. They braid red
and blue copies of grey stone mosaics.

Once you crawl through the tombs, watch
bats in the Crucifix Room loosed
by the guide's lamp, and the chamber where
the trove called "Stag's Interment"
with the famous golden sacrificial knives
was plundered by native archaeologists,

you rise to the lunar stone, encrusted
with blood too old to be red, symbols
on the walls that comprehend (the key
is gone) each sky movement. Then
you stand abruptly above ground
in a tiny ballcourt where seven women

pull red from the dust. "Sacrifice
of hearts in this place . . ." Turn
to the women who weave for the tribe
or tourists. All the hours of a day
sold cheap. What can they do but weave
sun carpets with the dust?

Malinche Eagles

Malinche eagles are, in tilting,
light — like seagulls, only with no cry;
and down gorges, blue-black, echoing
the creak of wings off damp walls.

The Indians consider them death-birds
that land on men and animals almost
dead and peck them accurately, deep.
Pinions are buried always in a grave
for death is a place of dismemberment.

Those birds symbolized the sun-kings,
who wore long robes of plumage
borne by pages up stone temples, where
flint beaks fed strong men to the sun.

Still east and east, the pathways
of the gorge overflown by those enormous
wingspans, six-foot, above
each turned stone, unstepped temple,
where donkeys trudge with firewood.

Whether deity embodied, or just
another carrion bird, see how like
reptiles in the stone they slough
to sunlight and become the sky.

Flown Eagle

As a little boy, the eagle seemed a possibility.
No — not that owl-like, mangy
bald beast the zoo served up with pruned talons.
I saw it as a seabird, hulking, wing-span
that if it came to perch on an ocean
liner would sink the sea in down.
Air whale. The sky was frightened of it.

But the crow is more magnificent (magenta, black,
amber all at once) than even the rock
eagle I saw paddling over Iowa — so small
someone had to point it out. I must have dreamed
some other genus — certainly, so far as I recall,
my eagle did not scream like that Iowan bird,
silent ate only big fish off the sea.

I have had to dispose of eagles, and the
things they seemed to touch: sky,
liner, and the deserted sea.
Which leaves me smaller territory,
even briefer dreams, never soft with strong
comforting birds — but other beasts more real:
hunter, adder, hare, and one blue unicorn.

Summary of the Eagle Theme
for Simon Chester

I told you as much (not much) as I know
about eagles: first, how they are omens,
especially among the Indian tribes. The Aztec
chose an eagle's cactus-island for his settlement
and called it by the serpent eagle's name;

and made the bird a god. He made it man as well,
called his last king "falling eagle" like the sunset,
when Toledo steel sliced Mexico from sea to sea.
Then I told you how the eagle was a psychopompos,
the "carrier of death into the sky", who

among the ancient Malatu of Chiriako
bore dead men to the moon, lined its nest
with stars, and made its chalk-white eggs
be meteors. It was intimate with the structure
of the sky, and sometimes perched on the wrist of god.

When it snatches up a living man — and brings him
back again — it leaves him blind and speechless,
for its claws are the trenchant wisdom of the owl,
its wings sea wings the height of sea-terns',
and its cry shriller than the man-o'-war's.

The eagle itself I have left to itself, a bit
timid to call it a bird — history like it possesses
drives like a spear, and can hit home,
and can leave you speechless.

Footnote on the Eagle Theme

I thought I'd done with eagles and
their progeny — until last night I found
a footnote. Let me describe it to you
in thin cloud, a flat moon, the burrow
of my pet hare under an acacia.

It was all Descartes' doing: he saw
us chopped off from our bodies into
thought and theorems. Those eagles who
fall on our passionate hares illustrate
his idea of intellect, the abrupt spite

and hunger from a cloud. No allegory
for my pet, clawed and hacked efficiently,
digested on the wind. Whatever huge mind
made us lame, infected flowers, found
animals could be cruel as a logical maw,
shouted in the eagle's passive beak, "You
are a predator!" — and made him so.

I expected this slaughter would make me forget
the symbol bird, my enormous paraclete.
But it fell with such cold intellectual fire,
the literal bird made me forget the hare.

Cotopaxi

for John and Marilyn Schmidt

Cotopaxi is this crater
where mountain lions retire from the hunt,
so high in rock no weed ever drew water here —
and rough. You wonder how a barefoot lion
walks the hot obsidian flints —
until you know he comes this way to hide.

Here too the Indian hermit served his raingod,
Tlaloc, far from cloud, conjuring
absent spirits of rain more potent
than any thunderhead. In this cave
you read on walls emblems of a worn-out
mystic: phalluses and flowers,
beside dry lightenings cut in stone:

ten years' concentration went to this,
under the star of "burning lizard", the days
of "divine tortoise". Some sherds, some bones,
and angular in shadows the fanged, dry-eyed god.

These things are parcel
of another faith from ours. They burn
with accumulated sunlight if we touch.
We come by a new calendar, our raingod
wears a cross — and yet
at evening, soft padding, bearded lions come,
in their teeth very old bones
we could choose to recognize.

Convento del Carmen: Mummies

Faience is walked colourless
down central corridors, the red and yellow
marrow of the flowers, dull. Through a cloister
and a fountain of raw gold-fish, light passes
in its sharp and silver forms that blind
the things they touch. Even in the long
mummy-room, through a high window,
light, transfixing an old exhibition.

A mother superior in sack-cloth, who appears
to have been corpulent has fallen forwards,
her face rests against the glass,
suspended like a dead fruit, unrevived by sun.
The body did not suffer until now, prevented
from acacias it admired and would have fed.
Choiring still, dead mouths hang always open
in an O as lips dry back on bone.

This lady of no skin but parchment eyeholes,
and the writing all in age, is called Carmen,
after the convent saint, or Latin song
the birds still make on faded tile.
Now the mouth that Ave'd, like a sucker
holds to the glass,
like the mouth of a fish, for sunlight.

Carlotta at Borda
for Olivia Harris

Momentum makes an empress. Work! Forget the heart,
the heart, those palaces and parks of Europe.
"We of the new world build a modern empire. Our formal
gardens undertake the unpatterned shade of big trees,
native flowers beaked and taloned like wild birds."

Power rose in her, its tulip cupped her heart —
unscrupulous but beautiful; and swans
mated on the lake, thrusting their magnificence
among pleasure boats. What did Cleopatra have
on this? — except a pyramid.

Peace in a barbaric country was not simply come by.
Recurrent measles (the pox, of course) took
imported courtiers, even for a time great
Maximilian. But one accomplishes
moments in the shade like calm.

My devil touches yours here, my hand the stone
you hold over generations. But even now
the devil longs for peace too imperial:
each Indian cowers to uphold it, and you —
invisible ghost rumoured within stone walls.

PART V

SOME FACTS

"Down fell he ..."
Drayton

If a Frog can Swallow its Eyes . . .

I missed my train. At least
I didn't miss the journey home,
but waited an hour for the six o'clock.

In that time, I sat conceiving how Ulysses,
missing boats at every port, had ten years
of this. I organized his progress in my eye:

the Troy he left, forever ugly ashes;
breathless women, sorceresses, strewed
his homeward route like petals after wind;

Ithaka so changed, at first a dog alone
recognized him through the smell of oceans,
recalled the tract of time, and died.

Those harbours were not —
he had forgotten — all air and sun,
but stone,

unfriendly ships and storms moored there.
Penelope, at least, perched faithfully like some
grey amorous bird in the famous wedding tree.

When I had seen him through,
for half an hour I prepared a private Odyssey
of my eye. Like the frog,

I thought how blinking I could send
my eye deep, to investigate
my own Mediterranean.

I sing its climb from the hideous
citadel above the nose; its course
through the esophagus

past the crashing cords that make the voice,
its sojourn with an alveolar Circe
in breezes of the lung, and finally

its shocking Ithaka, it reached
the heart where noone was at home.

Shipwreck

He was cut off at high-sea
leaving incredible jetsam
to the sand, where a widow picks.

The man salt water kills is still
thirsty. Piers record him — initials
of ship and sailor martyrs — tatoos
on log that drown at each high tide.

Fish are quicker than lime on a body —
think of that — his bone is shell
already, the mólusc, barnacle.

Hospital Garden

Roses then: August crutches.
Hyacinth laced with brown, kindled —
bees collide or peck at fire.

Designing afternoons, the nurses park
blankets, chairs and faces in the shade.
Inseparable from flowers, old fingers
pulse, lift with eyes red roses.

Desire so little; talk is out of place.
Bees are more articulate in movement
on bitter hyacinth, stale lavender.

Achieving no stillness inside a desire
silenced, unreconciled but bloodless,
spines throb and no word pushes
onto lips, but scent

of lysol. The garden is
not plundered, is cold as
black clay in the Summer wind.

The Gardener

If she looked at a place too long
it was to make a necessary symbol.
This garden is the product of her looking:
a maiden bench that tricks the rose
and violet, a conspicuous sundial,
and in the fronds of willow
a fountain with a slanting spout.

All with her own hands — and nonchalantly placed
under shrubs and cultivated cowslips, statuary relics
of her journeys — a little David, and St. John
reduced among toadstools. Keeping it in order and alive

she never sits shaded to consider
her handiwork, as any self-respecting
god would do, but tasks herself like Eve
after the apple fell, to keep her mind
from the fact — she had not been a life.
In Wellingtons, a neighbour child makes
shortcuts through her sprouting iris beds.

A Lady in her Seasons

She looked at minnows, propping a lepidopterist's
net on her knee — or with a tiddler net watched
the butterfly. When out for air she fell in love
with reflections on the light — those dragonflies.

And then, the way a boy will, she loved
her mirror best, the angle of her head. Tree
reduced to coiffure, and the eyes, miracle fish
under eyelid butterflies.

Then like a woman she took her body on
with her own hands, setting contemplation
aside. She held her breasts and waist just right
and knew her thighs a first time with her palms.

She is found unlike her gentle self would find —
not contemplated, but her fish and wings
possessed, breasts, the body of a watcher
become a place for delving and away.

Again, and several times. Noons are wintry
and the stream-ice stiffens fish, the butterfly
replaced by brown bats. Once more
she contemplates — no dragonflies but dragons.

Alligators in Florida
for Dinah von Reutter

Alligators in Florida come into old ladies'
back gardens, drinking flakes of grass
and firmly lodging on a lawn or among
rose-trees. No way to dislodge them
with their fine teeth. Always too
a wind from the woods, paper hurled
against wire, caught on wire teeth.

Low things elude fences. It's the moon
big with dust a fence keeps out, not
the slow progress of a reptile from the marsh.
All help out of reach in a Sunday of bells.
Old ladies must wait until teatime
watching with a thought:

my son was a giant, he would twist
that thing in two. Or
they watch the phosphorous
pepper tree the reptile
nuzzles and chews. Finally
the men come on broken flowers,
take it on, this Summer night.

An Old Lady

An old lady said to me when
I dug graves at Highgate, "Not-yet
is a model. Look how the yews
swell with almosts! To be
is the poem for a day after death."

I saw her ugly funeral too.
Eloquent, the oldest parson
worded her out of memory. A white
moth flew who was the soul.

I was Flora, lifting back
the sod, putting this
hideous daughter to bed.

In sleep she became Dutch tulips
and the blue forget-me-not.

Jellyfish

To live in a face like that!
one item in or out of an epileptic
ocean, now a sandclot, now
wide-spread like fishnet on the sea.

Adaptable to tides, it burns green or blue
as the wind blows. Polyps synthesize
neither coral nor conche — parasitic
on the suck and swirl of water,
camouflaged as water.

When, garbed in snorkle and aquatic glasses,
you see the jellyfish from underneath,
they are sea-spiders, doubtless, casting
web-like shadow on the seabed,

and each has a dense mucous core,
sprawling its force loosely in its arms;
these transparent tentacles suck a fish dry
in a minute, or sting the swimmer
with invisible teeth.

That sort of face needs no friends.
The lonelier, the deeper out it lives,
the better. But for a diver come up stung
it's fun to see one, snot-dry, grabbed on shingle.

The Fall

The tree is pruned, more fascinating
to dogs. The hedge is laid by man
as if the wind — here the grouse
and woodhens are more comfortable.

The serpent took my mother
in the wild growth. That was
an unsafe time before the secateurs
and lawning, when nature showed
bare haunches, like a dream.

We drive the wildness deeper
as we prune. It finds a burst
in sudden buds, the hollyhock
shoots up a broken galaxy.

And my father with a gun
has cured the woods, beat paths,
collected antlers. We have ranged
everything for comfort and facility.
Performed like wind.

Winter brings old and relaxing curves
of snow we cannot emulate, but break
with shovels, roll snow men
to beat them down with spades.